Samsung Galaxy Manual for Beginners and Seniors

The Advanced Step-By-Step User

Guide to Completely Setup and

Configure your New Device

Lizzy Newland

Table of Contents

INTRODUCTION

Are you new to the Samsung Galaxy A16 5G or helping a loved one get started with it? Look no further! This beginner-friendly, easy-to-follow guide by **Lizzy Newland** is designed specifically for **first-time users and seniors**, taking the guesswork out of learning your smartphone.

From unboxing your Galaxy A16 5G to mastering its most powerful features, this book walks you through every essential step:

- Simple setup and device layout
- Charging tips and battery-saving tricks
- Managing SIM cards and memory cards
- Navigating apps, notifications, and lock screen features
- Using the camera, gallery, and video modes like a pro
- Making calls, sending messages, and managing contacts
- Personalizing your phone with themes and settings

- Activating security, biometrics, and emergency features
- Utilizing Smart Switch to transfer data
- Exploring Google and Samsung apps
- Managing digital wellbeing and parental controls

Whether you're brand new to smartphones or just want to better understand your device, this comprehensive guide offers **clear instructions, helpful tips, and real-world solutions** in an easy-to-read format.

No technical jargon. No confusion. Just a confident start with your Samsung Galaxy A16 5G.

Get your copy now and take control of your smartphone journey today!

Caution

- To prevent any potential harm to your ears, it is sensible to refrain from playing media files or using speakerphone when holding your device close to your ears. Instead, opt for using the speakers of your device when making phone calls or adjusting your speaker settings.

- To maintain the integrity of your camera lens, it is advisable to steer clear of intense light sources such as direct sunlight. Prolonged exposure to strong light has the potential to harm the image sensor of your camera, resulting in unsightly spots or blemishes in your photos. It is crucial to note that once the image sensor is damaged, it cannot be fixed, rendering replacement an unattainable solution.

- Once the repairs have been completed at a Samsung Service Center, it is imperative that you only utilize your device if its acrylic body or glass remains intact. Failure to do so may result in potential harm while operating the device if it happens to be broken.

- It is important to note that the presence of foreign substances or dust in your microphone, speaker, or receiver can have a negative impact on the sound quality of your device and even lead to potential damage. It is crucial to avoid using sharp objects to remove these materials, as doing so can result in both physical harm to your device and a less aesthetically pleasing appearance.

- This can potentially result in issues with connections and battery performance.

- Dropped connections or reduced battery life can be attributed to problems arising from the aforementioned conditions.

To ensure optimal usage of mobile data or calls, it is very necessary to avoid any obstruction of your device's antenna caused by objects or hands.

- When connecting a metal case cover to a device, it is necessary to use a screwdriver.

- To ensure optimal device performance, it is advised not to affix metal stickers onto the antenna region of any electronic device.

- To ensure the proper functioning of sensors, it is advisable to utilize a screen protector that has been approved by Samsung. Using approved screen protectors eliminates the risk of sensor malfunctions.

- When exposed to high levels of humidity or submerged in water, the functionality of your touch screen may be rendered ineffective.

Samsung Galaxy A16 5G Device layout

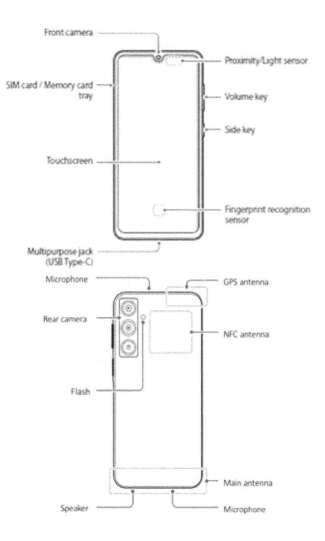

Front camera

Proximity/Light sensor

SIM card / Memory card tray

Volume key

Side key

Touchscreen

Fingerprint recognition sensor

Multipurpose jack (USB Type-C)

Microphone

GPS antenna

Rear camera

NFC antenna

Flash

Main antenna

Speaker

Microphone

Setting up Side key

To enter an exact feature or application, just double press your Side key.

To access your desired option, navigate to the Advanced features section in your Settings app, specifically the Side key menu.

Soft buttons

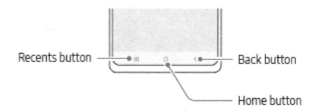

Recents button — Back button
Home button

Immediately your display is enabled, buttons will appear at the bottom of your screen. To access additional information, simply refer to the navigation bar, also referred to as the soft buttons, which will automatically appear.

Chapter 1
Charge your battery

It is very necessary to charge your battery when it is either new or has not been used for an extended period of time.

To protect your device and personal well-being, it is imperative to utilize Samsung-endorsed batteries, chargers, and cables. Employing an incompatible charger, cable, or battery not only jeopardizes the health of your device but also poses a risk to your own safety.

- If you fail to properly connect your charger to your device can result in substantial harm to both. Please note that warranty claims for damage caused by improper connection will not be accepted.

- To accomplish optimal outcomes, it is recommended to utilize the provided USB Type-C cable when connecting software updates. Connecting with a Micro USB cable poses the potential risk of causing harm to your device.

To save energy, it is recommended to pause your charger when it is not actively charging. Additionally, to prevent power drainage, it is advised to disconnect the power cord from your charger when it is not in use. It is important to keep your charger readily accessible and in close proximity to the outlet while it is charging.

Wired charge

To power the battery, connect the USB cable to your USB power adapter and then insert the cable into the multipurpose jack of the device. Immediately the battery is completely charged, disconnect the charger from the device.

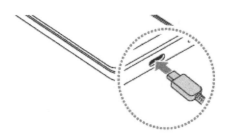

Fast charge

- To enter your favorite features, navigate to the Settings app and select Device Care, followed by Battery, and then Charging. From there, you can enable the features of your choice.

- To utilize the fast-charging feature, it is recommended to employ a battery charger that is compatible with adaptive fast charging.

While the device is charging, it is not possible to activate or deactivate this particular function.

If your device or screen is not turned on, the charging speed of your battery can be significantly increased.

Reduce your battery consumption

With your device, you have the advantage of multiple options that can assist in conserving battery life.

- Use the maintenance features on your device to enhance its performance and optimize its functionality.

- If the device is not being utilized, simply press the side button to power off the screen.

- Activate the energy-saving mode.

- Ensure to shut down any applications that are not needed.

- When you are not using the Bluetooth feature, please ensure that it is turned off.

- Deactivate the automatic synchronization feature for applications that necessitate synchronization.

- It is sensible to decrease the duration of the backlight time.

Helpful tips for charging batteries

- When the battery life has been fully depleted, it is important to note that the device will not power on immediately upon connecting it to the charger. To ensure optimal functionality, it is advisable to allow the device to charge for a brief period before attempting to turn it on.

- When you are using multiple applications simultaneously, web applications, or applications that rely on a connection to another device can result in a quicker depletion of your battery. It is sensible to use these types of applications when your battery is fully charged to prevent any interruptions in power during the transfer of data.

- When you opt to use a power source other than the charger, such as your computer, the charging process may be slower due to a decrease in current.

- Actually, it is likely to use your device while it is being charged, it is important to note that doing so will result in a lengthier charging time required to completely replenish the battery.

- When using an unstable power supply, it is possible that your touchscreen may experience functionality issues. Should this occur, it is recommended that you disconnect your charger from your device.

- Throughout the charging process, both your device and charger may experience heat. It is important to note that this is a normal occurrence and should not have any negative impact on the performance or lifespan of your device. However, if you notice that your battery is warmer than usual, it is possible that your charger may cease charging.

Before charging your device, ensure to thoroughly dry the multifunction jack.

- If your device is experiencing charging issues, it is recommended to bring it to an authorized Samsung Service Center for assistance.

Chapter 2
Turn your device on and off

It is important to adhere to all instructions and cautions provided by authorized personnel in zones where the usage of wireless devices is prohibited, such as hospitals and airplanes.

Turn on your device

In order to power up your device, all you need to do is press and hold the side button for a brief duration.

Turn off your device

1. To off your device, what you need to do is press and hold down the side button. Instead, you can also enter the notification panel and press ⏻the proper option.

2. Tap close

To initiate a device restart, simply press the Restart button.

Initiating a force restart

In the event that your device becomes unresponsive and freezes, you can resolve the issue by performing a restart. Just press and hold down both the Volume Down button and the Side button at the same time for a period of 7 seconds.

Emergency mode

Activated in times of crisis, emergency mode is a crucial feature that ensures immediate response and action.

If you want to minimize battery usage, activating emergency mode is an effective solution. This mode restricts specific features and apps. With emergency mode enabled, you have the ability to configure emergency alerts, share your precise location with others, place emergency calls, and access additional functionalities.

In order to engage emergency mode, all you need to do is firmly press and hold the side button. Following that, select the option for Emergency Mode. Alternatively, you can access the notification panel and tap on the arrow to navigate to ⏻ Emergency Mode.

To activate Emergency Mode, click on the ⋮ button labeled "Turn off Emergency Mode".

The remaining usage time is contingent upon the operational circumstances and configurations of your device.

Chapter 3
USIM or SIM card (nano SIM card)

You can insert two USIM or SIM cards, which enables you to have two phone numbers or two different service providers on a single device, that is if you have a dual SIM model. In certain areas, if you insert two SIM cards instead of one, the speed of data transfer might be slower. Additionally, please note that depending on your service provider, there may be certain services that require an internet connection that may not be accessible.

How to correctly install a SIM or USIM card

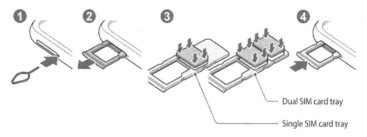

Dual SIM card tray

Single SIM card tray

For you to free the tray, you will need to insert the ejector pin into the adjacent hole.

Carefully pull out the tray from its nominated slot.

Please make sure that the gold contacts are facing downward on the tray to rightfully insert the USIM or SIM card. Carefully press the USIM or SIM card onto the tray to firmly secure it in place.

Put the tray back to its designated slot.

To use a Nano SIM card

- Just ensure that you do not misplace or allow anyone else to use your USIM or SIM card. It is important to note that Samsung cannot be held liable for any inconvenience or damage that may arise from the theft or loss of these cards.

- To avoid any potential damage to your device, it is crucial that the holes and pins are positioned at a perfect right angle to each other.

- When a SIM card is not properly inserted into the slot, there is a risk of it dislodging or being ejected from the slot.

- To avoid any potential damage to your device, it is crucial to ensure that the tray is always dry before plugging in your tablet, especially if it has come into contact with moisture.

- In order to safeguard your device from liquid damage, it is crucial to ensure that your tablet is completely inserted into the designated tablet slot.

SIM card manager (dual SIM models)

To enter the SIM Card Manager, open your Settings app and navigate to Connectivity, then select it.

- To use and personalize your SIM card, make sure to activate it and adjust its settings accordingly.

- With the activation of two SIM cards, users have the option to select a preferred SIM for specific functions, such as voice calls.

Memory card (microSD card)

The device's memory card capacity may differ depending on the model, and compatibility with the device is not guaranteed for all memory cards due to variations in memory card type and manufacturer.

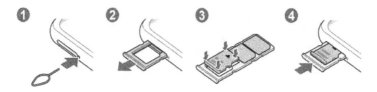

1. Insert your thimble into the adjacent slot to release the tray.

2. Gently pull out the tray from the slot.

3. To correctly insert the memory card, ensure that the side with the gold contacts is facing downward as you place it on the tray. Then, with a gentle push, securely position the memory card into the designated compartment.

4. The tray slot is where the tray should be refunded.

• It is very necessary to be aware that not all memory cards are appropriate for use with your phone or device. If you use a memory card that is not compatible, it could potentially cause damage to your card or device, and it may also result in the corruption of any stored data.

- Take advice as you insert the memory card in the correct orientation, ensuring that it is facing upwards.

- To avoid any potential damage to your device, it is crucial to ensure that both your thimble and hole are perfectly aligned.

- When succeed removing your tablet from the device, the mobile data connection will automatically be deactivated.

- If your memory card is not properly secured, there is a risk of it falling out or becoming dislodged from its compartment.

- It is important to ensure that your trays are thoroughly dry before inserting the tablet to avoid device damage.

- For you to avoid any liquid spills on the device, ensure that the tablet is completely inserted into the designated slot.

- If the file system of the inserted card differs from the supported exFAT and FAT file systems on your device, there is a possibility that your device may not be able to detect the card or request you to reformat it. In order to utilize the memory card, it is necessary to format it. Should your device encounter difficulties in recognizing or formatting the memory card, kindly reach out to a Samsung service center or the manufacturer of the memory card for assistance.

- The lifespan of a memory card can be significantly reduced by the constant process of writing and erasing data.

- Upon inserting a memory card into the device, the file directory of the memory card will be visible within the My File → SD Card folder.

How to properly remove a memory card

For you to carefully remove the memory card, it is very necessary to unmount it before proceeding with its removal.

For you uninstall, navigate to your Settings app, then click on Device Care, followed by Storage, Advanced, SD Card, and finally, Uninstall.

To ensure the protection of your device and data, it is very necessary to refrain from disconnecting external storage devices, like USB flash drives or memory cards, while in the process of accessing or transferring data, or directly after completing a transfer. Doing so can result in damage to your device or external storage, as well as the loss or corruption of data. It is crucial to note that Samsung does not provide coverage for any losses, including data loss, that occur as a result of improper usage of external storage devices.

How to properly format a memory card

There is a possibility that memory cards formatted on a computer might not be suitable for use with the device. To ensure compatibility, it is recommended to format the memory card directly on the device or smartphone.

To format your SD Card, navigate through the Settings app and click on Device Care, followed by Storage, Advanced, and finally SD Card.

To ensure the safety of your valuable data stored on the memory card, it is crucial to create a backup before proceeding with the formatting process. It is important to note that any data loss caused by user intervention is not included in the manufacturer's warranty.

Samsung account

By utilizing the integrated Samsung account service, individuals gain access to a wide range of Samsung services across their mobile devices, as well as Samsung websites and TV platforms.

To view the range of services available through your Samsung account, simply visit account.samsung.com.

1. To start, navigate to the Settings application on your device and go to Accounts & backup. And then choose Accounts and proceed to add a new account by choosing Samsung account.

Additionally, you have the option to access the Settings application and simply press ⊖ the designated button.

2. If you happen to possess a pre-existing Samsung account, you will be able to proceed with the signing-in process.

• To proceed with logging in using your Google account, simply click on the option that says "Continue with Google.

- In the event that you do not possess a Samsung account, simply click on the option to create one.

Resetting password or locate your ID

To retrieve your Samsung account when you might have forgotten your password or ID, you can just move to the Samsung account login screen and simply click on the options for Find ID or Reset Password. By providing the necessary details, you will be able to successfully reset either your ID or password.

Signing out of Samsung account

Once you have signed out of your Samsung account, any data stored on the device, including events and contacts, will be automatically erased.

1. To begin, open your Settings app and navigate to Accounts & backup. From there, select the Accounts option.

2. To sign out of your Samsung Account, go to Personal Information in the settings and tap on Sign Out.

3. To complete, choose the Logout option and type in your Samsung account password, then simply press OK.

Transferring data you're your previous device (smart switch)

Transferring data from your previous devices can be easily accomplished using the smart switch feature.

The Smart Switch feature allows the unified transmission of data from one device to another, certifying a smooth transition from the previous device to the latest one.

To enter the Smart Switch feature, just start your Settings app and go to Accounts & Backup and then tap on it.

- This feature may not be supported by all computers or devices.

- Copyright is a matter of great importance to Samsung, and as such, there are certain limitations in place.

How to transfer data wirelessly

Utilize the functionality of Wi-Fi Direct to seamlessly transfer data wirelessly between your old and new devices.

1. Turn on Smart Switch on your previous device.

In the event that you do not possess the application, you also have the option to conveniently download it from either the Play Store or Galaxy Store.

2. To start the procedure, just launch the Settings application on your smartphone and move to Accounts & Backup. And pick Smart Switch.

3. It is advisable to position the two devices in close proximity to one another.

4. To transmit the data from your previous device, simply navigate to the Send Data option and select Wireless.

5. On your previous device, make sure to tap the "Allow" button.

6. To initiate the transfer process, simply tap on your phone to select the desired items to bring and then proceed to tap on "Transfer".

Using external storage to backup and restore data

Utilize an external storage device, like a microSD card, to facilitate the transfer of data.

1. To ensure the safety of your data, it is important to transfer it from your old device to an external storage solution.

2. To start the procedure, enter the Settings app on your device and move to the section labeled Accounts & Backup. And proceed to select Smart Switch, followed by the option to Restore.

3. Simply adhere to the prompts displayed on your screen in order to transmit data stored on the external storage device.

4. Please ensure that you transfer the backup data from your computer.

Transfer backup data from your computer

To facilitate the transfer of data between your computer and device, it is necessary to download the computer edition of the Smart Switch app from the official Samsung website at www.samsung.com/smar tswitch. Prior to importing the data to your phone, it is imperative to first back up the data from your previous device onto your computer.

1. To acquire Smart Switch, visit www.samsung. com/smartswitch and download it onto your computer.

2. To begin, access the Smart Switch application on your computer.

In the event that your previous device was not manufactured by Samsung, it is recommended to utilize the program provided by the device manufacturer in order to safely back up the data on your computer. You need to use the USB cable that came with the smartphone to connect your previous device to the computer.

3. Follow the instructions displayed on your computer screen to create a backup of the data stored on your device.

Chapter 4
Understand your screen

Discovering ways to effectively manage your touchscreen.

Press and hold down your finger on the screen to enable the desired function.

Control the screen

Tapping

Tap the screen.

Touching and holding

Touch and hold the screen for approximately 2 seconds.

Dragging

Touch and hold an item and drag it to the target position.

Double tapping

Double tap the screen.

Swiping

Swipe upwards, downwards, to the left, or to the right.

Spreading and pinching

Spread two fingers apart or pinch on the screen.

1. To activate the desired function, simply press and hold the screen for approximately two seconds.

2. Perform the action of dragging and tapping twice.

3. To move the item to your preferred spot, tap and hold it two times before dragging the screen.

- To prevent any potential issues with your touchscreen, ensure that it is not in contact with any electronic devices. Electrostatic discharge can cause malfunctions in your screen.

- In order to prevent any potential harm to the screen, it is advised not to tap it with sharp objects or exert too much pressure with your fingertips.

Touch input near the edges of the screen, outside of the designated touch input area, may not be recognized by your device.

Navigation bar (soft buttons)

The soft buttons on the navigation bar provide a user-friendly interface for easy navigation.

Upon activating the display, a series of gentle buttons will materialize within the navigation bar situated at the lowermost part of the screen. The default configuration of your softkeys consists of the Back, Home, and Last buttons. However, it is important to note that the functionality of these buttons may vary based on the specific application being utilized or the prevailing conditions of its usage environment.

Button		Function
⦀	Recents	• Tap to open the list of recent apps.
○	Home	• Tap to return to the Home screen. • Touch and hold to open the **Google Assistant** app.
‹	Back	• Tap to return to the previous screen.

Hiding the navigation bar

Hide the navigation bar to access apps or view files on a larger screen.

To begin, open your Settings app and navigate to Display. And also find the Navigation Bar section and pick it. Next, choose Swipe Gestures under Navigation Type. Once you've done this, your navigation bar will vanish and gesture cues will become visible. For additional options, click on more and choose the option that best suits your preferences.

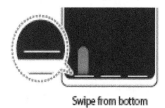

Swipe from bottom

Swipe from sides and bottom

To disable gesture cues and hide them from the bottom of the screen, simply click on the Gesture cues toggle.

Apps screen and home screen

The Home screen serves as the central hub for accessing all the features of your device. It provides convenient shortcuts to apps, widgets, and various other items.

On your Apps screen, you will find icons for all of your applications, including recently installed ones.

Switch between your applications and home screen

To enter the Applications screen on the Home screen, just simply swipe either up or down.

You can swipe either upwards or downwards on the Applications screen if you want to return to the Home screen. Alternatively, you can utilize the back or home button to achieve the same result.

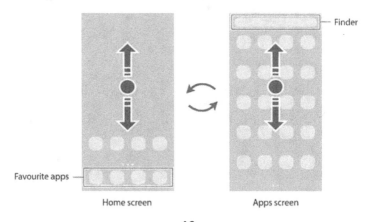

Favourite apps

Finder

Home screen   Apps screen

Once the Applications button has been successfully incorporated into your home screen, a simple tap will grant you access to the Apps screen. To start the procedure, look for an empty space on your Home screen and press and hold it down. This action will prompt a menu to appear, where you should select the option labeled "Home Screen Settings." Within this menu, you will find a radio button labeled "Application Keys." Tapping on this button, you will be able to complete the initiation process. As a result, the Apps button will be seamlessly added to the lower section of your home screen.

Displaying all apps on home screen

To showcase all of your apps on the home screen without utilizing additional app screens, you have the option to customize the home screen's layout and display. Simply click and hold on an empty space or access the Home screen settings, followed by Home screen layout, and then Home screen only. Finally, apply the changes to ensure the updates take effect.

By simply swiping left on your home screen, you can conveniently access all of your applications.

A helpful resource for beginners navigating the Finder app is "How to Launch Finder app".

Find content on your device with a quick search

1. To locate a particular app, all you need to do is open your notification panel and browse through the displayed options. Following that, access your applications menu by selecting the Search option, then scroll down and tap on Q.

2. Results can be obtained by searching through the various apps and content accessible on the device.

When users select additional content, they can find more information by conducting Q a keyboard search.

Transport items via the item box

To relocate an item, simply press and keep your finger on it until you can transfer it to a different spot. In case you want to move the object horizontally, just release it and drag it towards either side of your screen.

The process of swiftly adding apps to the Home screen is quite simple. By pressing and holding any app on the Apps screen until a checkbox emerges, you can effortlessly accomplish this task. Once you release the app, it will promptly make its appearance on the Home screen.

Create via the File -> New Folder menu option

The option to create folders can be found in the File menu, under the "New Folder" selection.

By grouping apps into folders and utilizing similar apps, you can efficiently organize and swiftly access them.

In order to relocate an app, simply use your fingers to drag it and position it over another app. Locate either the Home screen or Apps screen on your device and carry out this action.

New folders are generated for the chosen apps. Modify the name of a folder by selecting it and inputting a different name.

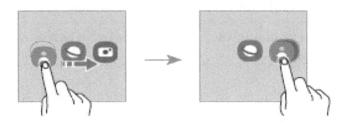

Move app from any folder

In order to relocate an application, simply press and hold the button while dragging it to the desired location.

Delete a folder

Specific procedures must be followed in order to delete a folder.

When using a Mac, if you press and hold a folder on the desktop, a prompt will appear asking if you want to delete the folder. Alternatively, you can right-click on the folder and select the option to delete it from the contextual menu. The contents of the deleted folder will be relocated to the Applications folder.

lock screen

When a phone is locked, the lock screen is visible to the user.

When the Side key is pressed, your device will automatically enter sleep mode, effectively locking the screen after a specific period of inactivity. In the event that your device remains inactive for a prolonged duration, the screen will automatically lock upon being touched.

Upon starting your screen, simply drag in any direction to gain access to its content.

To promptly activate your screen, utilize the Side key or opt for a double-tap on the display. Conversely, if your screen is already illuminated, a simple press of the Side key will promptly deactivate it once more.

Change your lock screen method

Navigate to the Settings app and select the option to modify your lock screen method. From the displayed menu, make your desired selection for the screen lock method and confirm by pressing OK.

By establishing a biometric data password, PIN, or pattern as your lock screen, you have the ability to safeguard the confidential information stored on your device. Each time you wish to access your device, an unlock code must be entered in order to proceed.

If you repeatedly enter an incorrect code, your device may reach the lock-out limit, causing it to reset and attempt another code. To access the Settings application, find the lock screen option and go to the secure lock's settings section. After that, select your desired method for unlocking the screen when it is locked. Once you have made your selection, navigate to the Auto factory reset option to restore your security settings.

Indicator icons

The icons used as indicators provide crucial information that is vital to understanding the subject being discussed.

At the top of the screen, you can view these widely recognized status icons.

Status icons

Battery full	Charging	Mute	Vibrate

Airplane	modeBluetooth active	Location active	Alarm

Notification icons

Missed calls	Call in progress	New message	Voicemail

New email	Download	Upload	App update

- In some instances, the status bar may not be visible at the top of certain app screens. If this occurs, you can easily find the status bar by either swiping downwards from the top of the screen or dragging it towards the bottom of the screen.

- When notification panels are opened, they selectively show specific indicator icons.

- Depending on the specific model and service provider, various indicator panels will be displayed.

53

Screenshot

To snap a screenshot, you need to use a screen capture program.

To capture a screen shot, begin by powering on the device and simultaneously pressing the Volume Down key and Side key until the screen momentarily illuminates. The camera roll, which can be reached through the Volume Down key, is made accessible by the Side key. Once taken, the screen shots can be found in one's Gallery.

Certain applications and software have the ability to prevent the recording of screenshots.

Panel notification

A dedicated panel designed specifically for the purpose of showcasing notifications.

Users have the ability to access the notifications panel in order to gain further insights into their indicator icons. This can be achieved by simply opening the status bar notification panel.

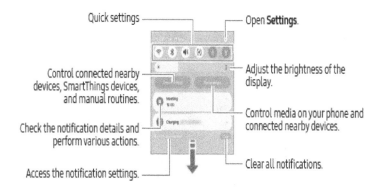

In order to view your status bar notifications, simply slide it downwards until a distinct blue line becomes visible. Conversely, to dismiss your notification panel, pull the status bar upwards until a noticeable white line emerges.

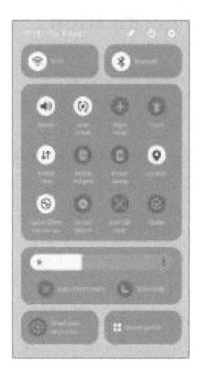

By utilizing the notification panel, you have the ability to unlock and explore a range of added features.

Chapter 5
Enter text

Keyboard layout

A keyboard will automatically display, when you want to enter your text.

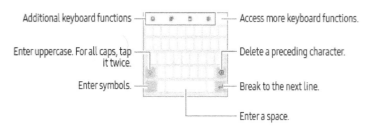

Additional keyboard functions — Access more keyboard functions.

Enter uppercase. For all caps, tap it twice. — Delete a preceding character.

Enter symbols. — Break to the next line.

Enter a space.

You have to change the input language to a supported languages to enter a text because text entry may not be allowed in some languages.

Additional keyboard features

- ☺ : Enter emojis in the app.

- 😀 : Enter stickers.

- GIF : Add animated GIFs to your collection.

- 🎤 : Text can be entered by using your voice.

- ⚙ : Change keyboard settings from anywhere.

Additional functions can be accessed by pressing the keyboard keys labeled

- 🔍 : Ask for input and incorporate it into your content.

- 🔳 : Enter text into the translator using the input fields provided.

- ⟨ˆ⟩ : Locate the text field in the program interface and open it.

Some features require specific model or service provider information.

Google Play Store

Download the app to make a purchase

Search for apps in the Google Play Store app using specific keywords or view the app catalog by category.

Choose ≡ Settings → Auto update applications from the menu and change the options.

Accessing apps in the launcher
Remove or disable apps from your device

Select any option by holding the app and pressing delete key.

- To remove an application, uninstall it from the download menu.

- If you disable this setting, default applications cannot be uninstalled from the device.

Not all apps allowed this feature.

You can change access to other apps by following these steps

Under the Settings application, choose the Disabled tab and pick the app you like to activate.

Change an application's default permissions

Before an app can function properly, it must request permission to access information stored on the device.

You can open settings for a specific application's permissions by clicking → ▼ → Application in the application's Permissions window. From there you can select an app and view its current permissions.

Setting app permissions

You can also change permissions by clicking Change Permissions.

To access Permissions Manager to change app permissions, open the Settings app and search for "Apps." After selecting the ⁝ app, find the permission manager and select any permission.

These applications require permission to fully function.

Chapter 6
Contact

Introduction

Professionally begin and cultivate new connections on your personal device.

Include additional individuals in your contact list.

The process of generating a fresh contact is as follows

1. Start your Contacts application and touch ⊕.

2. Choose any location that you prefer.

3. Provide the necessary details regarding the contact and then proceed to save the information by tapping on the designated button.

Import contacts

You can add contact by importing it from other storage devices to the device.

1. Launch your Contacts application and tap ≡ → Manage Contacts → Import or Export Contacts → Import.

2. Simply follow the on-screen instructions.

Sync contacts with web accounts

You can synced contact on your device with online contacts stored in a web account, such as a Samsung account.

1. Open the Settings app, click Accounts & Backup → Accounts, and select the account you want to sync.

2. Click Sync Account and then click the Contacts radio button to complete activation.

3. Tap → Sync Settings and then click ⋮ the Contacts radio button to complete activation from your Samsung account.

Search for contacts

Open your Contacts application. Touch Q from the top of your contact list and type in your search criteria And tap your contact. And you can perform one of the following:

- ☆ : Add to your favorite contacts

- ☏ : Make a voice call.

- ▣ / ▣ : Make a video call.

- 🗨 : Compose a message.

- ✉ : Compose an email.

How to delete a contact

1. Start your Contacts application and tap ⋮ →
   Delete.

2. Select a contact and click Delete.

How to share contacts

Contacts can be shared with others using various sharing options.

1. Launch Contacts application and touch ⋮ → Share.

2. Select the contact and click Share.

3. Choose any sharing method.

Create your group

Groups can be added just like friends or family, and you can use groups to manage your contacts.

1. Launch Contacts application and touch ☰ →
   Groups → Create Group.

2. Just follow the on-screen directions to create a
   group.

Merge your duplicate contacts

If your contact list contains duplicate contacts, you can merge them into one to optimize your contact list.

1. Start the Contacts app and tap ☰ → Manage Contacts → Merge Contacts.

2. View your contacts and click Merge.

Chapter 7
Telephone

Use your phone to make voice or video calls.

Make calls

1. In the Phone app, tap Keyboard.

2. Enter any phone number.

3. Touch on the 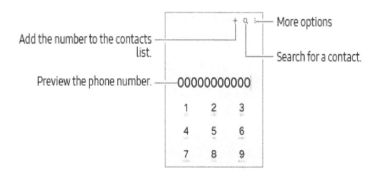 symbol to perform a video or

   voice call.

Add the number to the contacts list.

Preview the phone number. ——00000000000

More options

Search for a contact.

1	2	3
4	5	6
7	8	9

Make a call from your contact list or log entry

To make a call, tap the Recents or Contacts tab of the Phone app and swipe right on the listed contact or phone number to connect.

After viewing the Advanced Features section of the Settings app, click Actions & Gestures. Then turn on the "Swipe to talk or send message" option to activate the feature.

Engaging in international phone conversations

1. To access the Keypad feature within your Phone app, simply click on the designated option.

2. To increase the number of digits, simply press and hold the o button until a plus sign emerges.

3. After inputting your phone number, country code, area code, and the unique identifier for the software program, proceed by clicking on the next button.

Accepting incoming phone calls

The process of answering a phone call

Drag ⊙ the phone from the large circle to responds to a call.

Declining incoming phone calls

Drag ⊙ the cursor through the outer ring.

In order to decline an incoming call and send a message instead, simply slide the Send message bar upwards until it aligns with the Message textbox. From there, you can select the desired message to send.

To access the Settings menu on your phone, simply log in and click on the ⋮ → icon. From there, navigate to the Quick decline messages section and enter a personalized message. Don't forget to save your changes by pressing the designated button. Voila! You now have a variety of rejection messages at your disposal.

How to block phone number

One can easily access instructions on how to block phone numbers.

By simply adding specific numbers to the block list, it becomes possible to prevent calls from those particular numbers.

1. To block numbers on your phone, navigate to the $\vdots \rightarrow$ Settings app and choose the option labeled Block Numbers.

2. To input contact or phone numbers, simply click the Add Phone Number button and manually enter the desired number. Next, select either Recents or Contacts and choose a number. Finally, click Done to complete the input process. Alternatively, you can also select from previously chosen options by clicking on either option.

When a call is placed to a number that has been blocked, it will still be logged in the caller's call history. It is important to note that no notification will be received regarding this event.

To ensure that callers without visible caller ID are unable to reach you, simply block their numbers. Access the option to block unknown/hidden numbers and activate it.

Options during call

- Dial another number to initiate an additional call. Once your initial call concludes, the subsequent call will be placed on hold.

- In order to maintain a call, it is necessary to keep it connected.

- Once Bluetooth is enabled, you can seamlessly switch to your connected Bluetooth earpiece.

- To ensure proper usage of your speakerphone, it is important to maintain a certain distance between the device and your ear. Additionally, it is necessary to activate or deactivate the speakerphone when it is not being utilized.

- If you choose to mute your microphone, it effectively silences it and ensures that the person on the other end cannot hear your voice.

- You can choose to either close or open the keypad with the keypad/hide function.

- End the phone conversation ⌣ .

- When engaging in a video call, you have the option to disable your camera, preventing the other participant from seeing you.

- In the midst of a video call, you have the ability to effortlessly transition between the rear and front cameras.

The availability of certain features may vary depending on the model or service provider you have.

Chapter 8
Messages

Check your messages and send them via conversations.

You can request to receive or send additional messages while roaming.

Send Messages

1 Start the Messages application and touch 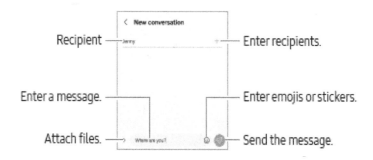.

2 Add recipients and enter your information.

3 To send a message, tap.

Recipient —— Enter recipients.

Enter a message. —— Enter emojis or stickers.

Attach files. —— Send the message.

View your messages

1. Open your Message application and tap on the Conversations.

2. From the message list choose a telephone number or contact list

• To reply to a message, click in the Your message input field, enter your message, and click 🔘.

• Kindly spread your two fingers separately to adjust font size.

Sort messages

Messages can be sorted by categories and easily managed.

Start your messaging app and press Conversations → New Category → Add Category. If you don't see the category option, press ⋮→ Settings and click the Conversation Category radio button to complete activation.

How to delete messages

Just press and simply hold down on the message you like to remove, then touch Delete.

Change your message settings

Launch your Messages app and tap ⋮ → Settings. You can change notification settings, block unwanted messages and other lists.

Chapter 9
Internet

Search for information online and bookmark your favorite sites for easy access.

1. Start your Internet application.

2. Enter the keyword or URL and click Go.

To display the toolbar, gently drag your finger down on the screen.

To easily switch between tabs, swipe right or left in the address bar.

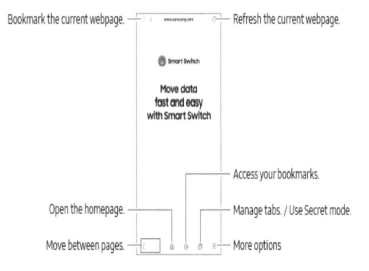

Bookmark the current webpage. — Refresh the current webpage.

Access your bookmarks.

Open the homepage. — Manage tabs. / Use Secret mode.

Move between pages. — More options

Use the secret mode

Setting a password for your Secret Mode prevents others from viewing your history, saved pages, bookmarks, and history.

1. Tap⬚ → Activate Secret Mode.

2. Click the Lock Secret Mode radio button to complete activation, click⬚ Start, and then set a Secret Mode password.

Secret mode changes the color of your device's toolbar. To disable incognito mode, click → Disable incognito mode.

In secret mode, some features such as: B. Screen recording cannot be used.

Chapter 10

Camera

You can snap pictures and record videos by using different settings and modes.

Etiquette when taking photos

- Note not to take photos or videos of other people without their permission.

- Note not take photos or videos that invade other people's privacy.

Photo

1. Open the camera application.

2. Start your application with a fast double-click ⬛ of the side button or drag the circle on the lock screen.

• Some camera features are not available after opening the Camera app from the lock screen, or when the screen is off but the lock screen method is enabled.

When your camera is not being used, it has the capability to automatically power off.

Depending on the model or service provider, certain methods may not be accessible. To focus the camera, 3. Simply click on the desired location after selecting the image on the preview screen.

To modify the brightness of the photo, simply tap the screen. Once the settings bar appears, you can adjust it by dragging **+** **−** it either towards or away from you.

4. Simply tap ◯ the screen to capture the image.

Settings

Zoom

Recording modes

Gallery

Switch cameras

Capture

- To avoid blurriness in videos or photos taken at a high zoom factor or resolution, it is important to maintain a reasonable distance from the subject when recording or capturing images.

- In the event that the image appears blurry, it is advisable to clean the lens of the camera and attempt another capture.

- To ensure optimal performance in modes that demand high resolution, it is imperative that your lens remains clean and free from any damage. Failure to do so may result in your device malfunctioning.

- The camera on your device is equipped with a wide-angle lens, which may cause a slight distortion in wide-angle videos or images. However, it's important to note that this distortion does not indicate any problems with the performance of your device.

- The amount of recorded video that can be stored may differ based on the resolution, resulting in varying maximum capacities.

To prevent condensation or fogging on your camera, it is important to avoid exposing it to abrupt changes in air temperature, as the temperature disparity between the inside and outside of the camera cover can cause this issue. In the event that fogging does occur, it is recommended to let your camera naturally dry at room temperature before capturing videos or snapping photos to ensure optimal clarity in the final result.

Utilization of the zoom features

There is option to either choose ✿ or ✿ drag left or right to adjust the zoom level on the screen. Another method is to use a pinching motion with two fingers - spreading them apart to zoom in and bringing them together to zoom out.

- ✿ : Capture the beauty of expansive landscapes by recording wide-angle videos or taking wide-angle photos, allowing you to preserve the grandeur of these locations.

- ✿ : By utilizing the wide-angle camera, you have the capability to capture regular videos or effortlessly snap uncomplicated photographs.

The zoom feature can only be accessed when utilizing the primary camera.

How to effectively utilize the camera button

- To initiate video recording, simply press and hold the camera button.

- In order to capture burst shots, simply drag the camera button to the edge of the screen and maintain pressure on it.

- To incorporate an additional camera, simply relocate it to any desired position on the screen and effortlessly capture images. Access the preview screen, tap on 🔅 "Capture Method," and select the "Floating Shutter" option to finalize the activation process.

The available options for current mode capturing

Please utilize the available choices displayed on the preview screen.

- ⚡ : You have the option to either disable or enable the flash.

- 🔅 : Adjusting the camera settings

Here are the necessary steps to make adjustments to your camera settings.

- Tap ⚙ on the screen preview to access various options. It's important to note that the availability of Choose the desired time interval for the camera to automatically capture a photo.

- 🖼 : Please choose the desired resolution and aspect ratio for the picture.

- 🎞 : Kindly choose an aspect ratio for the video.

- ✳ : Applying a beauty or filter effect is recommended.

- ◎ : Choose any measurement method. It depends on how the light value ◎ is estimated. Center weighting uses rays from the center of the image to calculate the exposure of the image. Spot estimates the exposure of a lens by using the light from the middle of the lens to focus. This matrix is used to average the entire scene.

- ⊙ : In FOOD mode, the subject within the circular frame should be in focus, and the image within the frame should be blurred.

- ✲ : Hue should be adjusted in FOOD mode.

Model and shooting mode determine the options available.

Picture mode

Your camera automatically adjusts shooting options based on your surroundings, allowing you to take photos with ease.

In the shooting mode list, tap Image, then tap ○ to take a photo.

Capturing your high-resolution images

Capture high-resolution images. High-resolution images can be cropped by enlarging the desired area and then saved as a high-resolution file.

From the shooting options, tap ▦ → ▦ and take a photo. The model determines the resolution.

83

Selfie

Take selfies by using your front camera.

1. Swipe up or down or tap the preview screen to switch to the front camera to take a selfie.

2. View the front camera footage

Touch 😎 to snap a selfie in wide-angle portrait or landscape mode.

3. To take a photo, tap ⭕

To apply beauty effects and filters

Before taking a photo, you can select filter effects and change facial features such as face shape or skin tone.

1. Click on ✳ the preview screen.

2. Select an effect and take a photo.

Lock exposure (AE) and focus (AF)

Exposure and focus can be locked in selected areas to prevent the camera from automatically adjusting to changing light sources or subjects.

To focus, click and hold on the area. An AE/AF frame will appear in this area, and your exposure and range settings will be locked. Even after taking a photo, the settings remain locked.

Movie mode

Your camera's recording options automatically adapt to your surroundings so you can record video with ease.

1. In the shooting mode list, tap ⊙ "Video" and then "Record Video".

- To snap picture while you are shooting, tap ⊚.

- While you are shooting, tap on where you like to adjust focus. To use autofocus, click AF to override manual focus.

2. Click ■ to stop recording video.

Live focus mode

You can use your camera to take photos with a blurred background but a clear subject.

1. Click Live Focus in the shooting mode list.

2. Drag the blue background adjustment bar to adjust the blur level.

3. When Ready appears on the preview screen, tap ○ to take the photo.

Background blur adjustment bar

- The following situations may cause background blur to not work:

- Movement of your device or subject.

- Transparent or thin body

- Background and theme colors are similar

- Simple background or theme.

Professional grade

Capture an image while manually adjusting various shooting options such as ISO or exposure value.

From the list of shooting modes, tap More → PRO. Select options and make settings. Then click "Take a photo".

Available options

- 🔘 : Select ISO value. This controls the camera's sensitivity to light. Bright or stationary objects have lower values. This value is higher in dim light or fast-moving objects. However, high ISO values can lead to image noise.

- 🔘 : Select a good white balance for the image to show the true color range. Color temperature can be adjusted.

- 🔘 : Adjusting the exposure value. This feature manages the volume of light the camera sensor obtains.

Separate Exposure Area and Focus Area

The exposure area and focus area can be separated.

Click and hold on the preview screen. The frame should be dragged to the area where you want to separate the exposed and focused areas.

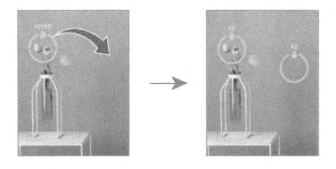

Panorama mode

Panorama mode enables you to snap a series of pictures and then tack them together in one giant scene.

1. From the recording mode list, just click on more → Panorama.

2. In one direction just click ◯ and sluggishly move the device.

Your photo should remain in your camera's viewfinder frame. If your thumbnail goes outside the reference range or you don't move your device, your device will stop taking pictures.

3. Click ⊙ to stop taking photos.

Don't take photos with blurry backgrounds, such as: B. Flat walls or empty skies.

Food pattern

Capture food pictures with vibrant colors.

1. In the recording mode list, just click on More → Food.

2. Click on the screen draws a circular box over the highlighted area.

To resize a circular frame, drag the corners of the frame.

3. To make adjustments, simply tap ⊕ and drag the gradient adjustment bar.

4. Capture a photo by simply tapping ◯ on the screen.

Macro mode

The macro mode feature allows for close-up photography with enhanced detail and clarity.

Capture detailed photographs of various objects from a close range.

To access the Macro shooting mode, simply navigate to the More option on your list of shooting modes and click on it.

Decorative photo mode

The option to activate the Decorative Photo Mode allows for the enhancement of visual aesthetics.

To access DECO PIC, simply tap on More from the list of capture modes.

Photo

To execute a desired action, simply slide the shutter to the edge of the screen after dragging the camera button, holding it in place.

Film

- Video Size for Rear Camera: Choose from various resolution and aspect ratio options for recording videos with the rear camera. Opting for a higher resolution will result in better video quality, although it will consume more storage space.

- To snap with your front camera, just select the aspect ratio for the front video size. Opting for a higher resolution when capturing video will undoubtedly enhance its quality, although it is important to note that this choice will also require a larger amount of storage space.

Useful functions

- Capture photos with vibrant colors and accurately portray intricate details in both shadowed and illuminated regions using the Auto HDR feature.

- Personalize your device by configuring it to save preview pictures captured with the front camera without the need to flip them.

- When selecting subjects, gridlines can be displayed in the viewfinder to serve as guides for framing pictures.

- In areas where the GPS signal is impeded, such as low-lying areas, between buildings, or during inclement weather, the strength of GPS character may diminish.

To prevent your location from being displayed on your photo when you upload it online, it is important to deactivate your location tag settings.

- To expand your recording options for capturing videos or capturing pictures, consider selecting additional recording methods.

- The camera will retain certain settings, such as shooting modes, even when turned on again, ensuring that the preferences you previously used are preserved.

- If you are snaping picture, note to incorporate a watermark at the lower left corner.

- You have the option to reset your camera settings if needed.

- Feel free to get in touch with us through our contact form, where you can ask any questions, you may have or access our comprehensive list of frequently asked questions.

- Explore the legal details and version of the camera application to gain insights about its functionality. Keep in mind that certain

Chapter 11
Gallery

Manage videos and images stored on your device by utilizing stories or organizing them into albums. Access and organize your media with ease.

The gallery is a versatile space that offers a multitude of opportunities for showcasing artistic works.

Use your gallery

Launch gallery application

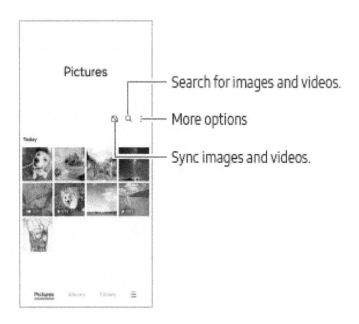

Organize similar pictures together

Access your gallery application and select images that are identical to each other, grouping them together. Then, take a moment to preview the images and choose only the best ones. Once you have made your selection, click on ⬜ the preview of the chosen image to view all the images within that group.

View your images

You can simply go to your gallery app and pick the pictures of your choice. To navigate through additional files, simply swipe the screen either to the right or left.

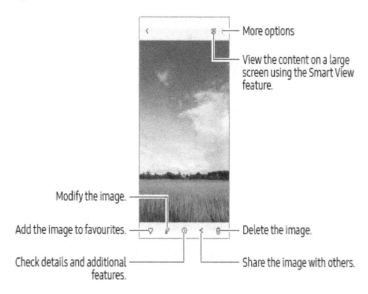

More options

View the content on a large screen using the Smart View feature.

Modify the image.

Add the image to favourites.

Delete the image.

Check details and additional features.

Share the image with others.

Resize the image to a larger scale

1. To begin, open your gallery application and choose an image from your collection.

2. To preserve a specific area, simply place your fingers on the desired location and give it a gentle tap ⬚.

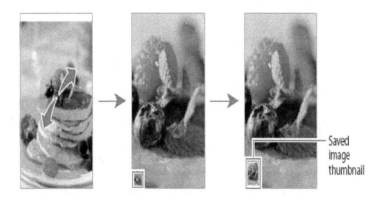

Saved image thumbnail

Album

Create photo albums and sort videos and pictures.

1. Enter the Gallery app and just click on the Albums →⋮→ Create Album to generate your image album.

2. Select your album, click Add Item and move your favorite videos or images.

Story

After you capture or save a video or image, your device reads location markers and dates, sorts videos and images, and creates stories.

Locate your Gallery application, simply click on the Stories, and pick any story.

To delete or add a video or photo, select a story and click Story Album ⦂→ Add or Edit.

View your videos

Start your google application and choose a video to watch. To watch other programs, swipe to the right or left.

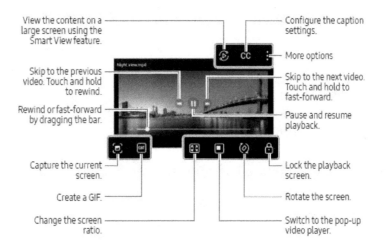

View the content on a large screen using the Smart View feature.

Configure the caption settings.

More options

Skip to the previous video. Touch and hold to rewind.

Skip to the next video. Touch and hold to fast-forward.

Rewind or fast-forward by dragging the bar.

Pause and resume playback.

Capture the current screen.

Lock the playback screen.

Create a GIF.

Rotate the screen.

Change the screen ratio.

Switch to the pop-up video player.

Samsung member

Samsung member customers have access to support services such as diagnosing device issues, and users can submit problem and error reports. Information can be shared with other users in the Galaxy user community, where you can check out the latest tips and news. Samsung members can help you solve any problems with your phone.

Calendar

You can manage your schedule by entering upcoming events in the planner.

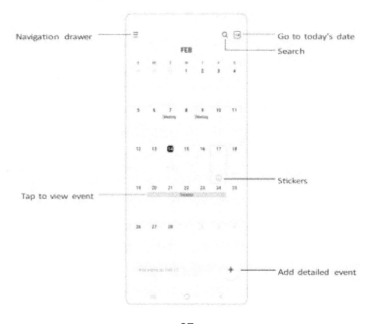

Create event

1. Launch the Calendar application and tap ⊕ or double-tap a date.

If you have saved a task or event for that date, click the date, and then click ⊕.

2. Please enter event details and click Save.

Memory

You can register tasks as reminders and receive notifications based on the conditions you set.

- Connect to a cellular network or Wi-Fi for more accurate notifications.

- To use location alerts, the GPS function must be enabled. Depending on the model, location alerts may not be available.

Activate reminders

Launch your Calendar app and tap → Reminders. Your Reminders screen will appear, and your Reminders app icon (🔔) will be added to your Apps screen.

Create memories

1. Launch your reminder app

2. Tap Write Reminder or ✚, enter the details, and tap Save.

Complete memory

Select a reminder from the Reminders list and click Done.

Restore memory

You can continue to complete the memory.

1. In the reminder list, tap ⋮ → Done → Edit.

2. Highlight the items you want to restore and tap Restore.

The reminder will be added to the reminder list and you will be reminded later.

Remove reminders from calendar app

To delete a reminder, select the reminder and click the Delete button. Multiple reminders can be selected and kept before placing a check mark next to each reminder. You can then press "Delete" to delete the selected memory.

Radio

Launch the broadcast app from anywhere.

You need to connect the headset to use its wireless antenna feature as an added feature.

When you start a radio station for the first time, available stations are automatically scanned and saved.

You can record audio from FM radio by scanning for stations and then saving.

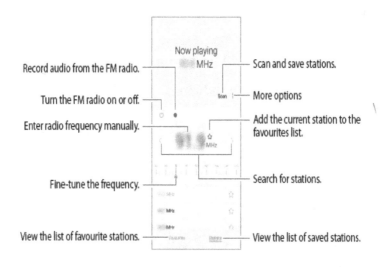

Record audio from the FM radio.

Turn the FM radio on or off.

Enter radio frequency manually.

Fine-tune the frequency.

View the list of favourite stations.

Now playing
MHz

Scan and save stations.

More options

Add the current station to the favourites list.

Search for stations.

View the list of saved stations.

Turning FM radio off or on

The frequency of your radio can by change by turning a knob on the radio.

Other settings are also possible

Add the radio stations you listen to the list by manually entering the frequencies.

Just focus on adjusting the station's frequency

- View a list of favorite channels.

- View a list of saved channels.

Apps are not available for some models and services.

Play on speakers

To listen to the radio with headphones, you need to connect speakers.

To play through your speakers, just tap⋮ on the link.

Record

To record voice memos or played back.

1. Open the Voice Recorder app in the App Store

2. Double-click ⬤ to start recording.

- Tap on the ⏸ "Pause" button labeled close to it to quit recording.

- When recording a podcast, add bookmarks to keep track of where you are in the episode.

3. Click ▪ the record button marked # to finish.

4. Click Save to enter a file name and complete the process.

Chapter 12

My profile

My Files is an application designed for the smartphone that conveniently stores both files and applications.

Open My Files app

The app allows users to access and manage various files with ease.

To access a file, simply open the My Files application.

In order to locate unnecessary files and folders, initiate the storage analysis process by selecting the Analyze button. This can be easily achieved by clicking on the Search button.

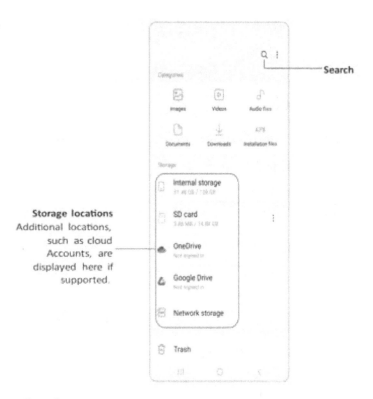

Search

Storage locations
Additional locations,
such as cloud
Accounts, are
displayed here if
supported.

Clock

Access the Clock app to establish alarms, observe time occurrences in various global locations, and determine their duration. Additionally, you can schedule events that will take place for a designated period of time.

Calculator

The process of calculations can encompass a range of formulas, both straightforward and intricate in nature.

Open the Calculator app from within the application.

- ⏱ : To access your past calculations, simply locate the history of your calculations. If you wish to remove this history, you can do so by selecting the Clear history button. To shut down the panel showing your calculation history, just click 🖩 on the designated button.

- 📏 : You can use the unit conversion tool to effortlessly transition values from one unit to another. This versatile tool enables the transformation of various measurements, such as length, temperature, or area.

Game launcher

Game launcher allows launching games from the application menu.

This app gives you quick access to games downloaded from Galaxy Store and Play Store. The app's game mode makes it easier to play games on your phone.

From the game launcher choose the game you like to play

- After accessing the Advanced Features section of the Settings app, navigate to the Game Launcher option and toggle the switch to enable it.

- By default, games you download from Galaxy Ware and Play Store will automatically appear in your game launcher. You can check if the game is loading by pulling out the library window and clicking the icon next to it.

Delete game from game launcher

After moving the library window to a higher position, press and hold the game title until the "Remove from Game Launcher" option appears. After clicking, release.

How to switch performance mode

Performance settings can be changed

In the Game Launcher application, select one of the available options. The list is located in the application's main menu bar. In this menu, find the ≡"Game Performance" option. Select this option and then choose one of the three available modes.

- To play your game optimally, focus on performance.

- This balances battery performance and usage time.

- When you play games on your device, power consumption is reduced due to the focus on energy conservation.

Game accelerator

Game accelerator can increase the speed of playing video games.

By downloading this software, you will be able to play games in an ideal environment and improve your performance. Additionally, you can take advantage of game boosters.

While playing a game, you can access the Game Booster control panel by clicking 🎮 on the lower right corner of the screen. Alternatively, you can pull up the bottom of the display to reveal the navigation bar. If your navigation bar is set up for swipe gestures, you can launch the notification panel. ⚙ : Change game accelerator settings according to your needs.

- Certain game features may be blocked while playing the game.

- You can prevent the navigation bar from moving by locking the buttons. Click 🔒 on the navigation bar to unlock buttons and move them.

- While playing a game, you can lock the touch screen by dragging the lock icon in any direction.

- Use the camera button to take a photo or screenshot.

- Click the ▣ Record button in the navigation bar to start recording your game session.

- You can change how the game booster panel opens by swiping it open in the navigation bar. By tapping "Block" you can toggle this gesture to activate the panel.

Each game offers different options.

Playing games with pop-ups to launch apps

While playing a game, sometimes a pop-up window opens in which an application is launched.

Select the application code by clicking ⬤ and viewing the options.

Share content

Sharing content is a common activity.

Find the different sharing options you can use when looking for shared content. These are examples of how to share images

1. Click any image in the Gallery app to open a window and select an option.

2. Click ⭐ Share using your preferred method.

Quick share

Discovering ways to easily distribute content among nearby devices.

1. To begin, open your gallery application and choose an image from your collection.

2. To activate the feature, simply swipe down on your notification panel on your secondary device and tap on ⊙ (Quick Share).

3. To transfer the image, simply tap on ⭐ "Quick Share" and choose the desired device from the options available.

110

Ways to locate individuals who can access your telephone

Enable the functionality for individuals to both send and locate items using their mobile devices.

1. To activate the feature, begin by accessing your notification panel. Then, swipe downwards and find the (Quick Share) option. Lastly, click ⊚ on it to successfully start the process.

2. Hold down your finger on the screen to enable the Fast Share feature.

Once you click, the quick share settings will promptly appear before you.

3. Kindly select any of the accessible choices.

- Only contacts: The option to exclusively share your contacts with the designated device.

- Enable the sharing feature on all devices in close proximity to your phone, allowing them to connect and share data.

Shared album

Generate a collective album that enables the sharing of videos and photos with fellow individuals, while also providing the convenience of effortlessly downloading any desired file. Establish collaborative albums to distribute photos or videos among others, allowing for the seamless retrieval of your files at any given time.

1. To begin, open your gallery application and select an image by tapping on it.

2. Access the Shared Album by tapping on it.

3. Feel free to choose any album that you would like to share.

To initiate the sharing of an album, simply tap on "Create Shared Album" and then proceed to follow the prompts provided in order to successfully create the album. To conclude the process, please ensure that you carefully adhere to the instructions displayed on your screen.

- Depending on the speed of your network, playing high-resolution video from your shared album may result in interruptions to your video connection.

- The maximum file size allowed for sharing in a shared album is 1 GB.

Samsung Global Target

In 2015, the United Nations General Assembly (UNGA) established the Global Goals, a set of objectives focused on fostering a sustainable society.

The power of these goals lies in their ability to combat climate change, address inequality, and eliminate poverty.

Join the Samsung Global Goals initiative and become an active participant in the global movement to create a brighter tomorrow. Discover more about the Global Goals and expand your knowledge through Google apps.

Google apps

Google serves as the driving force behind various types of apps, including those related to business, social interactions, and entertainment. It is worth noting that certain apps may require the use of a Google Account for access.

To obtain further details about each application, refer to the help section provided for each individual app.

- One such app is Chrome, which allows users to navigate the internet and conduct searches to gather information.

- Gmail: Utilize the Gmail platform to send and receive emails.

- Maps: Explore the global map, pinpoint your precise location, and access location details for nearby establishments.

- Experience the vast selection of videos and music available on YouTube Music through YT Music. Additionally, you have the ability to access and enjoy your personal music library stored directly on your mobile device.

- Enjoy Movies & TV: Explore a wide selection of TV shows and movies available for rent or purchase on the Play Store.

- Cloud Storage: Safely store your content in the cloud, giving you the freedom to access it whenever you want and easily share it with others.

- YouTube: Create and watch videos while you are sharing them with others.

- Photos: Edit, organize, and search for videos and images from various sources in one central location.

- Google: Speedily look for articles online or on your telephone.

- Duo: You can make simple video calls.

Some apps may not be available depending on model and service

Chapter 13
Setting up
Require device settings

Open your Settings app.

Click Q to use keyword search settings.

Connection
Options

Customize settings for different connections, such as:

B. Bluetooth and Wi-Fi functionality.

On the Settings screen, click Connect.

- Wi-Fi: You can simply activate the Wi-Fi feature to automatically connect to any Wi-Fi network and get into other network devices or the Internet. More information is available via WiFi.

- Bluetooth: Use Bluetooth to share media files or data with other Bluetooth-enabled devices. For more information, please contact Bluetooth.

- NFC and payments (available on NFC-enabled models): Set your device to read Near Field Communication (NFC) tags that contain

116

product information. This feature can also be used to pay and purchase event or transportation tickets after downloading the required app. For more information, see NFC and payments (for NFC-enabled models).

- Follow airline policies and instructions from aircraft officials.

- Mobile networks: Adjust mobile network settings.

When setting up your device's custom settings, log your data usage and set a limit on how much you can use. This prevents your mobile data usage from exceeding the limits you set. Once this limit is reached, your mobile data will be automatically turned off to save data.

- Data Saver protects applications from transmitting or receiving data in the background. For more information, see Data Protection Procedures.

- You can install apps that always use mobile data, even when connected to Wi-Fi.

- Go to "Setting up a dual-SIM smartphone" for additional information.

You can connect your phone to your computer or another phone to allow the two devices to share your mobile Internet connection. For more information, see Mobile Hotspot.

- Additional connection settings provide additional connection options.

Wi-Fi
Connect to a Wi-Fi network

1. After accessing the "Settings" page, find the "Connectivity → Wi-Fi" option and turn it on.

2. From the list pick a Wi-Fi network.

3. Networks with a lock symbol require a password.

- After connecting to power, your device automatically connects to the Wi-Fi network. This process can be stopped by changing the "Auto-reconnect" switch next to your network. This ensures that your device does not automatically connect to the network.

Wi-Fi Direct

Wi-Fi Direct allows transferring files directly between devices using direct line of sight.

1. After accessing the Settings screen, find and select the Connections option. Next, change the setting from "Off" to "On." This completes the process of turning on Wi-Fi.

2. Click anywhere on the screen to find the Wi-Fi Direct option.

More information about the identified devices can be found in the report.

3. A list shows all devices that the application can connect to. If the app can't find the device you're looking for, you'll need to enable Wi-Fi Direct on the device. If the devices both accept to transverse Wi-Fi Direct, they will be connected.

Bluetooth

Communicate with other devices via Bluetooth to share media or data.

- Samsung is not responsible for any misuse, damage, or data loss caused by Bluetooth.
- There should be no obstructions between devices that would reduce range.
- Devices that have not been approved or tested by the Bluetooth SIG will not work with your phone.
- Samsung is not responsible for any consequences related to illegal use of the Bluetooth function, such as: B. Wiretapping calls for commercial purposes or stealing files.

Pair device with another Bluetooth device

1. When accessing the Settings menu, click Bluetooth Connections in the main menu. After powering on, all detected devices will be listed. Choose one to pair.

2. When you are done checking the manual for the other device, just tap on the Bluetooth

pairing button on your desired device to make it visible in the list.

To establish a successful connection with a Bluetooth device, it is necessary for your device to accept a request for connection. This can be accomplished by accessing the Bluetooth settings menu on your device.

3. Immediately the both devices begin a Bluetooth connection request, they will start connecting. If you wish to disconnect paired devices, simply tap ⚙ on the Unpair button located beside the name of the device you intend to remove.

Sending and receiving data

Transferring data between devices can be accomplished by both sending and receiving. One simple method for transferring images to another device is through Bluetooth. This transfer protocol is supported by numerous applications, allowing for the sharing of various types of data, such as media files and contacts. The following steps serve as an example of how to send an image to another device.

1. Immediately the Gallery application is launched, select your desired photo. Just simply tap on the icon to choose the device from the Bluetooth list.

2. Please make sure visibility is on for the device you like to pair, if you notice that you can't see the device on this list when you ask to pair devices.

3. The demand to connect via Bluetooth should also be allowed on the other device.

NFC and payments (NFC-activated models)

To access information stored within NFC tags, which requires the use of a reader, users must first download the necessary applications. This enables them to utilize NFC-activated models for payments, such as purchasing transportation tickets or paying for events.

Careful handling of your device is essential due to the presence of a preinstalled NFC antenna, which is integrated within the device.

Read from NFC tags using the appropriate tools

1. Utilize the necessary tools to access information stored on NFC tags. Expand your knowledge by simply tapping NFC stickers. To complete the setup of your connection, navigate to the toolbar and click on the Settings icon. From there, select Connections and toggle the switch next to Payment and Near Field Communication.

2. For convenient visibility of its NFC tag, it is recommended to position the NFC antenna area on the rear side of the device.

Before you proceed with any data transfer or NFC tag reading, it is crucial to ensure that both the screen and lock buttons on your device are in the switched and unlocked positions. Failure to do so will result in your device being unable to receive data or read NFC tags.

Debit/credit cards available via NFC functionality

Before you can use NFC to pay your bill, you must first register for the mobile payment service. Ask your service provider for more information about their services or to register.

1. After accessing the Settings menu, click on the Connectivity option and toggle the NFC & Payments switch to enable it.

2. To access your card, press the back of your device against the card reader's NFC antenna.

3. To set the default payment application, go to the Settings tab and click on the Connect option. From there, select NFC and payment options, then select the specific app.

4. Certain payment applications are not included in the payments available on the Service.

File transfer may fail if two devices try to transfer data at the same time.

Data saver

Data can be transferred between two devices by touching them with their respective NMN antennas. This includes images and contact information as well as all other types of data.

Data saver feature enable

After accessing the Settings screen, select Connectivity → NFC & Payments. You can then toggle the switch to activate it.

Click the Android Beam switch on your device to complete activation.

You can connect another device's NFC tag to your device's NFC tag by placing the NFC-compatible device on top of another NFC-enabled device. A connection is established with just one click.

 If two devices try to send data at the same time, the file transfer may fail.

Users can use a smaller version of the application instead of the full version.

Make sure some background apps aren't using data by closing all open apps.

1. Under the Settings menu, just choose Connections > Data Usage > Data Saver.

2. Click the switch to turn it on.

When data protection mode is enabled, an icon appears in the user status bar.

3. Select an application from the list to use data without restrictions. Select Data Saver to activate the application. Then select each application.

Apps to mobile data only

Make sure to always use mobile data when connected to a Wi-Fi network. For example, your device can be set up to use mobile data only for apps you want to back up or streaming apps you can disconnect from. These apps use your mobile data even if your WiFi is not activated.

On the Settings screen, click Connections → Data usage → Mobile data apps only, click the switch to complete activation, and then click the switch next to the desired app.

Background

Click on the Wallpaper option in your settings screen to make adjustments to the wallpaper settings for both the lock screen and home screen.

Themes

To modify the appearance of your device, you can apply various themes that will alter the icons, lock screen, and visual components of your home screen. Simply navigate to the settings screen and select the "Themes" option.

Chapter 14
Security and biometrics
Options

Adjust settings to protect your device.

On the Settings screen, click Biometrics & Security.

- Face recognition: You can modify your device to recognize your face and simply unlock your screen.

- Fingerprint: You can also as well register your fingerprint to unlock the screen. For more information, see Fingerprints

- Biometric settings: Customize your biometric settings.

- Google Play Protect: Customize your device to scan for malicious behavior and malicious apps, receive notifications of future corruption and delete them.

- Security Updates: View your device's software version and check for updates.

- Search My Mobile: You can deactivate or activate the Search My Mobile feature. To check and track a stolen or lost device, visit the Find My Mobile website (findmymobile.samsung.com).

- Install unknown apps: Customize your device by allowing the installation of apps from unknown sources.

- Additional security settings: Customize additional security settings.

Some features may not be available depending on model and service provider.

Initial setting

Upon powering on your device following a data reset or initial setup, it is important to carefully adhere to the instructions displayed on your device's screen.

In the event that you are not linked to a Wi-Fi network during the initial setup process, certain device features may be inaccessible to you.

Lock screen

The lock screen is the initial screen that appears when waking up or unlocking a device.

Options

To personalize your lock screen, simply navigate to the Lock Screen option in your Settings and tap on it.

- You have the ability to personalize the security lock settings by customizing the screen lock method of your preference.

- Personalize your device by adjusting the settings for background services, including the dynamic lock screen.

- Modify the appearance of the clock on your lock screen by customizing its color and style.

- Enable the roaming clock feature to have your lock screen display both your home time zone and local time zone when you're in a different location.

- Personalize the settings for the items shown on your lock screen with the Face Widgets option.

- Personalize your device by adding contact information, such as email addresses, to be displayed on the lock screen.

- Lock screen details: Access legal information and lock screen version.

Smart Lock

The lock screen method you select will determine the range of options that are available. Smart Lock.

When a trusted device or location is detected, your device has the capability to automatically unlock and stay unlocked.

For example, if your home is set as one of your trusted locations, your device will recognize that location and automatically unlock when you arrive home.

Under the Settings screen, please do click the Lock screen → Smart lock, and go through the on-screen instructions to simply finish the setup.

- This function is available after setting the lock screen method.

- After turning on the device or not using the device for 4 hours, you need to use the preset password, PIN code, or pattern to unlock the screen.

Face recognition

Your device can be set up to use facial recognition to unlock.

- If you use your face as the screen lock method, you will not be able to use your face to unlock your screen the first time after turning on your phone. To use your device, you must unlock the screen using the password, PIN, or pattern you previously set when registering your face. Be sure to remember your password, PIN or pattern.

- If your screen lock method is changed to Slide or None, both methods are unsafe. If you change your screen lock method to Swipe or None, it is not secure and all your biometric data will be deleted.

If you want to use biometric data in features and applications, you must re-register your biometric data.

Face recognition guide

Before using facial recognition to unlock your device, please note the following:

- People or things that look like your photo can unlock your device.

- Passwords, PINs or patterns are more secure than facial recognition.

For good facial recognition results

When you are using the facial recognition, please take note of the following:

- During the registration process, it is important to consider specific conditions such as the presence of heavy makeup, a beard, a mask, a hat, or glasses.

- Prior to registering, ensure that the area you are in is adequately illuminated and that your camera lens is free from dirt or smudges.

- To ensure optimal matching results, it is important to ensure that your images are clear and free from blurriness.

Guide to register your face

To ensure optimal face registration, it is recommended to register your face indoors, away from direct sunlight.

1. To access the necessary settings, navigate to the Biometrics & Security section on your device and select Face Recognition.

2. Proceed by following the prompts displayed on the monitor, and then select the "Next" option.

3. Select a method for securing your lock screen.

4. Next, you can decide if you want to wear glasses and then proceed by tapping on the Next button.

5. Please position your face within the designated box displayed on your screen. Your camera will automatically scan and capture your facial features.

- If you are unable to successfully unlock the screen using facial recognition, select the option to Delete Face Data in order to remove your registered face, and proceed to register your face once more.

- Enhance the accuracy of facial recognition by selecting Add Alternate Appearance and adding another appearance to the system.

Unlock your screen with your face

You can use your face to unlock your screen without a password, PIN, or pattern.

1. Under the Settings screen, simply click on Biometrics & security → Face recognition.

2. Unlock the screen by using the simple current lock screen method.

3. Click the face unlock switch to complete activation.

4. On the lock screen, view the screen.

No other lock screen methods are needed to unlock after facial recognition. If your face is not recognized, use the standard lock screen method.

Guide to delete registered face data

Registered face data can be deleted.

1. On the Settings screen, click Biometrics & security → Facial recognition.

2. Tap Clear face data → Clear.

All related functions will also be disabled, once your registered face is removed.

Fingerprint recognition

In order for fingerprint recognition to function effectively, it is necessary to register and store your fingerprint information on your device. However, it is important to note that depending on the service provider or model, this feature may not be accessible.

- The security of your device is strengthened by utilizing the unique attributes of your fingerprint for recognition. The likelihood of your fingerprint sensor mistaking two distinct prints is minimal.

- When you set a pattern, PIN, or password when registering your fingerprint, your device will not recognize your fingerprint. In this case, you can register your fingerprint again. If you have a password, PIN, or pattern, you can reset your device by resetting it before trying to use it again.

- When using biometrics, if you no longer use touch or nothing as the lock screen method, you will need to re-register the app or feature. This will delete all previous biometric data and ensure new data is registered and used.

Enrolling your fingerprints

Improved fingerprint accuracy due to increased friction and pressure.

If you notice the following conditions, you may experience performance issues when scanning fingerprints on your device.

- Small or sensitive fingers will not register on your device.
- Enhancing the efficiency of fingerprint recognition can be achieved by registering the unique patterns on your hand, typically used for device operations. The built-in fingerprint sensor embedded in the side key is capable of accurately identifying your fingerprints.

For optimal performance, it is necessary to eliminate any obstructions, such as adhesive film or protective stickers, that may impede the functionality of the recognition sensor when utilizing a fingerprint scanner. The effectiveness of fingerprint scanners is enhanced when the recognition sensor remains uncovered by any supplementary accessories.

To ensure optimal functionality, it is important to refrain from leaving any fingerprints or smudges on the sensor. It is recommended to place your entire finger on the sensor for reliable recognition.

To prevent any potential issues, it is recommended to touch a metal object in dry climates before utilizing this feature. This simple action will help dissipate any built-up static electricity and should always be performed before using this feature.

Guide to register fingerprints

1. On the Settings screen, click Biometrics & Security → Fingerprint.

2. You can follow the on-screen commands and tap on Next.

3. Set any lock screen method.

4. Your fingers should be on the side buttons. Immediately the device recognizes your finger, bring it up and position it on the side button again.

This should be repeated until your fingerprint is registered.

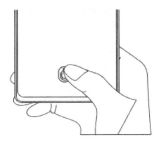

5. After completing the fingerprint input, click "Finish".

Click Verify added fingerprint to verify your registered fingerprint.

Unlock your screen with your fingerprint

You can unlock your screen using just your fingerprint, no password, PIN or pattern required.

1. On the Settings screen, click Biometrics & Security → Fingerprint.

2. You can simply place your fingerprint on the fingerprint sensor and scan while the screen is locked.

Delete the registered fingerprints

Registered fingerprints can be deleted.

1. On the Settings screen, click Biometrics & Security → Fingerprint.

2. Click on delete to remove fingerprint.

Chapter 15
Digital Wellbeing and Parental Controls

Manage your device usage with the help of parental controls and digital well-being features. Take control of your daily life by accessing your device usage history and utilizing tools to prevent interruptions. Additionally, you have the option to set up parental controls for children and effectively manage their digital activities.

By accessing the Settings screen, you also have the option to navigate to Digital Wellbeing & Parental Controls. Within this section, you have the ability to manage your screen time by setting a daily usage goal for your device.

- App Time Limit: Take control of your app usage by setting timers to restrict the amount of time you spend on each app per day. Once the set limit is reached, the app will be disabled, and you will no longer have access to it.

- Activate Focus Mode to eliminate any distractions from your device and concentrate solely on the task you are currently working on.
- Relax: Engage wind mode to alleviate eye fatigue and promote uninterrupted sleep.
- Manage Kids' Usage: Regulate your children's digital activities.

Device care

With just one click, you can optimize your device automatically using this convenient feature for device maintenance. It offers a comprehensive overview of the device's current system security, memory, storage, and battery status.

Optimize device

Navigate to the Settings screen and choose Device Maintenance to optimize your device.

From there, click on Optimize Now. By utilizing the Quick Optimizer feature, you can enhance the performance of your device through the following actions:

- Check for malware and malfunctioning apps.
- Address excessive battery usage.

To ensure optimal performance, the device can be configured to automatically optimize itself when not in use. To activate this feature, navigate to the Advanced settings and select Auto-optimize. Simply toggle the switch to enable it. If you prefer to specify a particular time for the device to perform automatic optimization, you can do so by tapping on the Time option.

Battery

Monitor the level of your battery and determine the remaining duration of usage. Activate the battery-saving feature to conserve battery life on devices experiencing low power levels.

1. To go in the Battery settings, access the Device Care section on the Settings screen and click on it.

2. Monitor Battery Usage: Keep track of how your device's battery is being used and conserve power by putting unused apps to sleep. Simply select the app you want from the list of installed apps and activate the "Sleep app" switch to ensure optimal battery performance.

3. Choose a power mode, such as power-saving mode, from the available options.

   - Manage app power usage by limiting battery consumption for apps that are not frequently used.

4. Enhancing Charging Speed: Optimize your device settings to expedite the battery charging process. For additional details, refer to the section on Fast Charging.

5. The duration of usage that remains indicates the amount of time left before the battery is fully depleted. The remaining lifespan is determined by the conditions under which the device is being used and the settings of the equipment.

6. You may experience a lack of notifications from certain applications that utilize power-saving mode.

Storage

Simply navigate to the Settings screen and enter Device Care to check the recent memory status of your device. From there, proceed to the Storage section. You can also clear space by uninstalling unnecessary applications or removing the files. Simply choose a category and select the items you wish to remove or uninstall. Finally, click on the Remove or Uninstall option to complete the process.

The advertised capacity of your device may not accurately reflect the available internal storage space due to the allocation of storage for default applications and operating systems. When your device undergoes an update, the usable capacity may be altered.

The Samsung website provides detailed specifications that include information about the available memory capacity.

Memory

To enhance the speed of your device, access the Device Care section in your Settings screen and navigate to Storage. From there, you can effectively prevent apps from running in the background by selecting an app from the list and choosing the option to Clean up now.

Security

By using this function, your device will undergo a thorough scan to detect any potential malware. The outcome of this scan will be presented to you, providing an accurate representation of the security status of your connected device.

To access the security settings of the app, navigate to the main menu of the app and tap on the Device Care option. From there, proceed to tap on Security and choose the Scan Phone option from the list provided.

www.ingramcontent.com/pod-product-compliance
Lightning Source LLC
LaVergne TN
LVHW051243050326
832903LV00028B/2547